# Endorsements

Dr. Tim Barker's new book, *It's Not All About Sitting at the Head Table,* is the revelation of a leader's heart and spirit who has been tried as by fire! It is one thing to lead based on ego and desire for "the mic" rather than understanding the private experience of leading with "the towel." Every leader who aspires to a higher-level position would be wise to prayerfully process the experienced heart of a leader who has led out of personal pain without becoming bitter or cynical. Instead, his reflection has been on the model of Jesus in His Servant Role in which He washes the feet of those who would grieve His heart. Vivid contrasts are drawn between the motivation of position and title as opposed to the motivations of service and love for others. Dr. Barker is a wounded healer, opening to others what it means to experience leadership that navigates the shadows of disappointment and the opportunities for public ministry. I personally know his story and the authenticity of every chapter in this message to leaders! *It's Not All About Sitting at the Head Table* is not pessimistic or a venting of leadership challenges, but an invitation to the ultimate goal of any Christian service! There is pain now, but glory then! There is suffering now, but the reward of leading with "the towel" when we stand in His presence!

Dr. Gaylan D. Claunch
Superintendent
North Texas District Assemblies of God

---

Tim Barker's new book is a short read that hits to the heart of a "prima donna" era of pastoring and ministry. Challenging the current leadership concept that elevates the leader, this book calls on those in ministry to remember they are merely servants called to wash feet and lead sheep. In the line, "In God's kingdom, honor is not measured by where you sit but by where you serve," Tim reminds us that we are not to seek positions but places to serve. This book will challenge you to pick up the towel and basin even as Jesus did. God has called no one to be famous. He has called all to be faithful.

James R. Braddy
Superintendent Emeritus
Northern California/Nevada Assemblies of God

This small book will commandeer your attention and grip your affections. Every chapter operates like a loaded spring: tight, compact, and ready to release life-giving energy! Tim's words will cause you to reflect, maybe shed some tears, and enhance your commitment to the towel.

Dr. Terry L. Yancey
District Superintendent
Assemblies of God Kansas Ministry Network

---

Dr. Tim Barker has given the Church a timely and practical gift in *It's Not All About Sitting at the Head Table*. In a world that often measures leadership by position and prestige, this book flips the script, reminding us that true greatness is found not at the head table, but at the feet of others. Whether you're a seasoned pastor, a young leader, or simply someone hungry to reflect Christ more fully, this book is a must-read.

Dr. D.E. Wootton
Superintendent/Network Pastor
Oklahoma Assemblies of God

# IT'S NOT ALL ABOUT

## SITTING
### AT THE
# HEAD TABLE

# Books by Tim Barker

*Anticipating the Return of Christ*

*At Your Feet*

*Called Camp 2025*

*Discovering God in the Secret Places*

*End Times*

*God's Revelation and Your Future*

*Mighty Men of Courage from the Bible*

*My Jesus Journey*

*My Jesus Journey: Crescendo*

*My Jesus Journey: Glissando*

*My Jesus Journey: Rhapsody*

*Names of God*

*Open Doors*

*Our Privilege of Joy*

*Reflecting Christ Through the Fruit of the Spirit*

*The Authentic Christian: Revealing Christ through the Fruit of the Spirit*

*The Call of Ephesians*

*The Lord with Us*

*The Twelve: Taking Up the Mantle of Christ*

*The Vision of Nehemiah: God's Plan for Righteous Living*

*Truth, Love & Redemption: The Holy Spirit for Today*

*Unified Church*

*Your Invitation to Christ*

# It's Not All About

## Sitting at the
## Head Table

# Tim R. Barker, D. Min.

Network Pastor/Superintendent
South Texas Ministry Network

IT'S NOT ALL ABOUT SITTING AT THE HEAD TABLE,
Barker, Tim.

1st ed.

ISBN: 979-8-9924875-2-7

# Dedication

*Servant Leadership and the Towel Test* was birthed from the powerful example of servant leadership I've been privileged to witness throughout my life. This message is especially shaped by the lives of pastors who didn't just preach servanthood—they lived it.

Chief among them were my father and brother, Fred Barker and Doug Barker, who were true servants of the Lord in every sense. I also owe a deep debt of gratitude to pastors like Carl Vaughan, LaVern Rodgers, William F. Sipes, A.W. Walden, Tom Shepherd, and J. Sidney Watson—each of whom modeled what it means to be faithful shepherds and trustworthy servants. Their legacy of humility and service continues to inspire me, and I will be forever grateful.

Tim R. Barker

# Contents

# Contents

# Introduction

The soloist on Sunday morning.

The evangelist who fills the local sports stadium.

The Christian author who receives award after award.

We want to be that person. The glitter and glamor pull us in, and we dream, "That could be me!"

Yet the story Jesus lived out in the Word says something very different. Our Lord modeled a lifestyle of service and working in the background to achieve His goals on this earth.

Here's what the example of Jesus teaches us:

branding isn't enough. Wearing the Christian name-tag is worthless if we don't hold up in the wash.

Do we feed the hungry? Do we clothe the naked? Are we a friend to the friendless and a comfort to the brokenhearted?

What's important to us, the glitter of proclaiming the Gospel or the grinding agony of time on our knees in prayer?

Jesus washed His disciples' feet. The Master stooped to the level of a servant, and in doing so, became a greater example of service than any soloist or evangelist ever dreamed.

The cost of leadership is heavy. The price for being "on show" rests hard on our shoulders.

Here's the lesson from our Lord:

To truly stand out in the Kingdom of God, we must first spend time on our knees.

## — I —

# The Lure of the Head Table

---

Everybody wants the spotlight, but not everybody is willing to endure the scars.

Walk into a wedding reception, and the energy is magnetic.

*Laughter fills the room.*

**Dresses shimmer.**

*The room is buzzing.*

But even with all the splendor, our eyes always drift to the head table:

- That's where the action is.

- That's where the power sits.

- That's where the cameras aim.

*It's instinctual.*

I remember being at a wedding where a sharply dressed guest, probably confident in his clout, slid right into the head table before the bridal party arrived. When the real VIPs arrived, the poor guy tried to vanish under the table.

His confidence crumbled faster than the centerpiece he almost knocked over scrambling to leave.

Here's the thing: He wanted ...

- Honor without invitation.

- Spotlight without sacrifice.

- Prestige without price.

And, if we're honest, that's the temptation we all face at times.

*Why are we wired like this?*

Why do we spend more time polishing our image than preparing our hearts?

It's not just a wedding thing. It's ...

- A boardroom thing.

- A pulpit thing.

- A ministry conference thing.

- A social media thing.

It's the subtle whisper in our soul that says: You belong at the head table.

But in the upside-down Kingdom of God, the highest seat isn't a platform – it's the floor.

The real symbol of status isn't a throne – it's a towel. Jesus didn't come striding in with a scepter. He stooped with a basin and water.

This is the Kingdom uniform! Not the microphone. Not the corner office. Not the reserved parking spot.

**It is a towel!**

In God's Kingdom, honor is not measured by where you sit but by where you serve.

When James and John (through their mother, no less) came with a bold request – "Jesus, grant us the head seats!" – they didn't realize what they were asking.

*"You don't know what you're asking,"* *Jesus replied. "Can you drink the cup I'm* *about to drink?"*

— Matthew 20:22—

They wanted the glory of the head table. Instead, Jesus was offering a cross-shaped sacrifice.

Are you chasing the applause of the crowd … or the approval of Christ?

Because if your ministry, your calling, your influence, or your platform is just a long audition for human admiration, you're sitting at the wrong table.

The true measure of spiritual leadership isn't how many followers admire you. It's how many of them are changed because you bled for them.

Jesus didn't audition for attention, He emptied

Himself. He didn't climb a ladder. He climbed up a hill, one called Calvary.

And from that hill, He didn't rain down judgment …

- He washed feet.

- He forgave enemies.

- He served the world with nails in His hands.

If we're going to wear anything in the Kingdom, let it be Jesus! Let it be service! Let it be humility!

**Let it be the towel!**

**Pray with me:**

*Jesus, when my ego wants the head seat, remind me of Your knees on the floor.*

*When I crave visibility, remind me that You chose invisibility to save me.*

*I trade applause for assignment. I surrender prestige for the privilege of washing feet.*

*Let me lead — not with pride in my chest — but with a towel on my arm.*

# — 2 —

# Clashing Kingdoms

---

There's a very real combat situation between the *World* and Jesus' *Model of Greatness.*

*Whoever wants to become great among you must be your servant.*

— Matthew 20:26 —

Let's be real. The world doesn't just disagree with the Kingdom of God …

It clashes violently with it.

*Two Kingdoms, Two Contradictions.*

**The world says:**

- "Climb to the top."

- "Be the loudest in the room."

- "Leverage your influence."

- "Build your brand."

**But Jesus says:**

- "Take the lowest place."

- "Be quick to listen, slow to speak."

- "Lay down your rights."

- "Deny yourself."

We're not talking about small differences — we're talking about a head-on collision between two completely different operating systems.

One fueled by self.

One surrendered to the Savior.

### Mama Zebedee's Bold Move

Imagine the scene in Matthew 20:20:

James and John's mother kneels before Jesus. But don't be fooled by the posture. This is a power play.

"Jesus, grant that my two sons may sit, one on Your right and the other on Your left, in Your Kingdom."

*Translation:*

"I want them seated in the spotlight. I want them next to the Throne. I want them recognized."

It's not just a mother's pride — it's worldly ambition masquerading as spirituality.

Jesus' response is thunderous:

"You don't know what you're asking. Can you drink the cup I'm about to drink?"

The question was very real. The cup wasn't gold-trimmed with royal wine.

It was bitter with betrayal.

It was full of sweat, blood and sacrifice.

In Jesus' model:

**Down is up.**

Let's paint a contrast:

**World System**

- Climb the ladder

- Be recognized

- Protect your brand

- Win the argument

- Sit in First Class

**Kingdom of God**

- Descend into service

- Be hidden in humility

- Lay down your life

- Wash the feet

- Give your seat away

You feel that tension?

*Good.*

You were never called to blend in. You were called to stand out by kneeling down.

**Let me further illustrate this.**

We've all seen the corporate grind.

- The intern becomes the assistant.

- The assistant becomes the manager.

- The manager becomes the VP.

- The VP becomes the corner office.

And the higher they climb, the further they get from the ground – and often, from the people.

But Jesus carried His own ladder ... one shaped like a cross.

**He didn't ascend to save. He descended.**

- Into the womb

- Into the stable

- Into the Jordan River

- Into the Upper Room

- Into the Garden of Gethsemane

*And, finally ... into grace.*

The world says, "Climb higher to lead more."

Jesus says, "Kneel lower to love deeper."

- Stop chasing titles. Start chasing towels.

- Stop polishing your nameplate. Start dirtying your hands.

- Stop waiting for a microphone. Start listening for the whisper of those in need.

- The greatest leaders in the Kingdom don't have entourages – they have callouses.

### Down Is Up!

Have you mistaken visibility for value?

Have you traded basin work for platform work?

Have you turned ministry into a race for influence instead of a rhythm of obedience?

When Jesus taught this lesson, He didn't post a tweet about servanthood.

He didn't drop a masterclass.

He got on His knees and washed feet covered in road dust and betrayal. He wasn't performing – He was pouring.

Greatness isn't how many people know your name.
It's how many burdens you lift when no one sees.

*Whoever wants to be first must be your
slave – just as the Son of Man did not come to
be served, but to serve ...*

— Matthew 20:27-28 —

**Pray with me:**

*Jesus, reverse my instincts.*

*Where I crave upward motion, pull me toward downward devotion.*

*Where I chase recognition, anchor me in responsibility.*

*Make me allergic to selfish ambition and addicted to humble assignment.*

*May the only elevation I seek be kneeling closer to You.*

# — 3 —

# The Weight of the Seat

---

## What Leadership Actually Costs

*"Not many of you should become teachers, my fellow believers, because you know that we who teach will be judged more strictly."*

— James 3:1 —

Let's talk about the illusion of leadership:

- Fancy titles

- Reserved seats

- Elaborate introductions

- Hotel upgrades at conferences

- Social media followers – i.e. digital applause

On the surface, leadership looks like perks and privilege.

But ask anyone who's actually carried a call from God, and they'll tell you: The seat may be elevated, but it's heavy.

## Head Tables Carry Weight, Not Just Visibility

At a wedding, if the chicken is undercooked, guests don't glare at the caterer – they look at the head table.

In ministry, when things go wrong, such as when a small group fractures, a program flops or a sheep wanders, eyes drift to the leader.

Leadership doesn't shield you from blame. It puts you in the line of fire.

Consider with me some leaders in the Bible:

### Moses:

Chosen to liberate a nation … but a man who was

constantly overwhelmed by the people's complaining.

*I cannot carry all these people by myself;*
*the burden is too heavy for me.*

— Numbers 11:14 —

**David:**

Anointed king ... but hunted by Saul. Slept in caves. Carried the guilt of personal failures. He wore the crown but often walked with a limp.

*David went out of the cave and called out*
*to Saul ...*

— I Samuel 24:8 —

**Paul:**

Wrote two-thirds of the New Testament ... yet faced persecution, spent time in prison, and was cast aside by many of the local church leaders. He even survived a shipwreck and worked to support his own ministry efforts. He said:

*I face daily the pressure of my concern for*
*all the churches.*

— 2 Corinthians 11:28 —

**Jesus:**

He carried the weight of the world on His shoulders – literally. Before He was crowned in glory, He was crowned with thorns.

*Jesus cried out in a loud voice ... "My God, my God, why have you forsaken me?"*

— I Samuel 24:8 —

### The Higher the Seat, the Heavier the Crown

You want the platform? Then embrace the pressure.

You want influence? Then prepare for the isolation.

You want the microphone? Then learn to live with the burden of bleeding silently while blessing publicly.

Leadership isn't about getting your way.

*It's about making a way.*

Leadership isn't a comfy chair at the head table.

*It's often the last one awake and the first one blamed.*

Leadership isn't being the face of the ministry.

*It's being the spine when the body wants to collapse.*

So, the next time you admire someone's mantle – don't covet their seat until you've wept over their scars.

Jesus didn't gain influence through applause – He gained it through agony.

If Jesus had to suffer before He reigned, why do we think we'll reign without sacrifice?

Do you still want the spotlight now that you know its weight?

Will you still say, "Yes," when leadership means you cry in private and serve in public?

Will you carry the weight when no one claps, reposts, or says thank you?

I don't just want the seat – I want the strength to carry it.

The towel isn't light. But it's holy.

**Pray with me:**

*Father, don't just anoint me – prepare me.*

*Don't just elevate me – fortify me.*

*Let me carry the burden of leadership with blood-washed hands and basin-filled love.*

*When I feel the crown of leadership grow heavy, remind me that You carried a heavier one first.*

*Make me faithful in the weight, joyful in the sacrifice, and anchored in the call.*

# — 4 —

# Jesus and the Towel Test

---

*Now that I, your Lord and Teacher, have washed your feet, you also should wash one another's feet.*

— John 13:14 —

It's Thursday night.

Jesus knows the cross is hours away.

The enemy has already whispered to Judas.

The Disciples are full of Passover lamb and delusions of grandeur.

*And then it happens ...*

The King stands up.

- Not to rally the troops.

- Not to rebuke the betrayer.

- Not to give a last-minute masterclass in theology.

He takes off His robe, wraps Himself in a towel, and grabs a basin.

He wears the tools of the lowest servant in the house.

And the Lord of Glory bends low and washes their feet:

- The feet of Peter – who would deny Him.

- The feet of Thomas – who would doubt Him.

- The feet of Judas – who would betray Him.

Our Lord didn't just teach servanthood ...

*He performed it.*

*Do you understand what I have done for you?*

— John 13:12 —

The question still echoes.

Because in one moment, Jesus redefined leadership forever.

- Not by grabbing a sword ...

- Not by writing a manifesto ...

- But by kneeling with a towel.

He flipped the definition of greatness with His actions of leadership.

Let's compare the difference between the rules dictated by worldly success and the rules of success in Jesus:

### Earthly Leadership

- *Be served*

- *Protect status*

- *Gain control*

- *Maintain image*

### Jesus' Leadership

- *Serve others*

- *Empty yourself*

- *Give sacrificially*

- *Carry a cross and a basin*

You might not be at a foot-washing ceremony this week, but the towel test is everywhere:

### The CEO

*Staying late to clean up after the team leaves.*

### The Worship Leader

*Unseen in the back row and praying over every chair before service starts.*

### The Youth Pastor

*Driving across town to deliver groceries to a family that left the church.*

### The Single Mom

*Worshipping with tears in her eyes as she folds laundry and leads her kids to Jesus.*

Towel-bearers don't need applause — they already

have purpose.

You don't need a microphone to be mighty.

*You just need a towel.*

• Jesus washed the feet of people who'd run away from Him.

• True leadership is not being recognized but being willing.

In some church cultures, we've created a warped definition of "servant leadership." We say servant ... but we mean celebrity pastor with a team of assistants.

We use the word humble ... but we want retweets and greenroom perks.

Let's detox the Body of Christ from performance leadership.

Let's rip the glitter off the stage and fall back in love with the glory of the basin.

I don't need a title – I just want to mirror the King who kneeled.

If Jesus can wash feet, I can carry the basin.

**Pray with me:**

*Jesus, break my addiction to being seen.*

*Let me serve like You – with no camera, no credit, no crowd.*

*Give me joy in unseen places.*

*May my name fade as Yours increases.*

*Make the towel my uniform and the basin my altar.*

# — 5 —

# The Marks of a Servant-Leader

---

### Humility, People and Faithfulness

*But among you it will be different. Who-ever wants to be a leader among you must be your servant.*

— Matthew 20:26 —

There are many areas of leadership out there.

Corporate leaders, social media content creators,

influencers, visionaries, and movement starters.

But not all of them carry Heaven's approval.

The Kingdom only recognizes one kind of leadership: that of the servant.

You don't become one just because someone hands you a mic, gives you a title, or adds "Pastor" to your email signature.

You don't earn the badge of leadership without paying the price.

Servant leadership is a work of the Spirit — it marks you, molds you, and often bleeds you.

### Humility over Hype

*God opposes the proud but gives grace to the humble.*

— James 4:6 —

### World's Model

- Self-promotion

- Image curation

- Branding over becoming

## Kingdom Model

- Self-denial

- Image-surrender

- Crucifixion over charisma

**If your platform is louder than your prayer life, you're not a servant leader — you're a performer.**

Real humility says:

- "Let them see Jesus, not me."

- "I don't need the best seat — I need a bowed knee."

- "I'm not too big to clean toilets or too important to stack chairs."

When was the last time you did something that didn't benefit you?

If it's been a while, the hype may be outpacing the humility.

## People over Position

*The Son of Man did not come to be served, but to serve.*

— Matthew 20:28 —

Leadership is not about managing people. It's about loving them well.

The danger of platform leadership is that we start to love the stage more than the sheep.

We hide behind emails, schedules, and assistants because it's easier to be important than to be interrupted.

But servant leaders don't lead from above ...

- They walk among.

- They're the first to the hospital room.

- The last to leave the altar.

- They are the one weeping over that young student who just got arrested.

Your title may be on the wall, but a servant leader's real ministry is developed in the mud ... *with the people.*

### Position Leadership

- "Protect the brand."

- "Command respect."

- "Enforce structure."

- "I'm too busy."

### Servant Leadership

- "Heal the broken."

- "Earn trust with love."

- "Build family."

- "People are the mission."

## Faithfulness Over Fame

*Well done, good and faithful servant ...*

— Matthew 25:21 —

Servant leaders don't chase likes. They don't measure impact by reach. They don't define success by being "known."

- They show up.

- They stay consistent.

- They stay hidden if that's where God puts them.

Listen … fame is fleeting, and most of it is fake.

God doesn't reward virality. He rewards faithfulness.

### Heaven's Hall of Fame

- The widow who gave two mites
- The woman who poured perfume
- The intercessor who fasted in silence
- The usher who opens the church doors at 6 A.M. every Sunday

You may never preach a sermon, publish a book, or trend on TikTok … but if you're faithful, Heaven takes note.

The greatest enemy to servant leadership is the desire to be seen before you've been shaped.

### Let the Lord:

- Break your pride
- Bury your ego

- Build your backbone

Then you'll be ready to lead with a towel instead of a title.

**I don't need credit to carry the Kingdom. I just need a clean towel and a surrendered heart.**

**Pray with me:**

*Lord, make me small enough to be mighty in Your hands.*

*Strip the stage from my heart and replace it with a basin.*

*I choose humility over hype, people over power, and faithfulness over fame.*

*Hide me in the secret place and build in me a heart that loves to serve — even when no one's watching.*

# — 6 —

# When Leadership Hurts

---

### Serving Through Betrayal, Burnout, and Brokenness

Each of these could be an entire book on its own, whether betrayal by a trusted church member ...

Burnout from overwork, over-commitment, or just not knowing how to say no ...

Or brokenness from a loss of relationship or from financial collapse.

Let's look at what the Psalmist has to say:

*Even my close friend, someone I trusted, one who shared my bread, has turned against me.*

— Psalm 41:9 —

Let's talk about the side of leadership that no one is posting about. Everyone wants the microphone, the moments, and the momentum. But few are ready for the heartbreak of leadership.

- Being betrayed by someone you mentored.

- Being misunderstood by the ones you served faithfully.

- Feeling invisible even while you're pouring out everything.

## Betrayal

Jesus certainly understands being wounded by a trusted friend. However, He didn't flinch when demons screamed. He didn't panic when storms threatened.

But betrayal – from the inside – cuts deep.

*Judas, would you betray the Son of Man with a kiss?*

— Luke 22:48 —

**Think about this:**

- Judas wasn't a stranger. He was a friend.

- He wasn't a critic. He was a follower.

- He wasn't outside the circle. He sat at the table with our Lord.

The people closest to our hearts have the most access to hurt them.

But Jesus still washed Judas's feet. Can you serve the ones who might betray you?

A young pastor once told me: "I thought the hardest part of ministry would be the spiritual warfare out there. I never knew the deepest pain would come from someone I trusted on my team."

*Betrayal is a knife that often comes wrapped in a handshake.*

But take heart — you're in good company.

Along with Jospeh, David, and Jesus.

- Don't let betrayal make you bitter. Let it make you braver.

- Don't let pain make you pull back. Let it drive you deeper into Christ.

- The towel still belongs in your hand, even when someone stabs you in the back.

Burnout is when you've given everything … and it's still not enough.

*I have labored in vain; I have spent my strength for nothing at all.*

— Isaiah 49:4 —

### Burnout

*Burnout whispers:*

- "Nobody notices what you do."

- "You're replaceable."

- "You're not making a difference."

Sometimes you pour out and still feel dry.

You lead with joy and end the night, exhausted and empty.

*Signs you're burning out:*

- You're irritated by people you once loved to serve.

- Your spiritual disciplines feel like chores.

- You fantasize more about quitting than pushing through.

- You feel like your calling has become your cage.

Let's be clear ... even servant leaders get tired.

*Healing strategy for burnout:*

1. Pull away before you break down. (Jesus often withdrew.)

2. Sabbath is sacred. Don't wear exhaustion as a badge of holiness.

3. Talk to someone. Silence feeds burnout. Community crushes it.

4. Drink deeply from God again. You can't pour out when your well is dry.

## Brokenness

The leadership-refining fire of servant leadership will break you.

Not to harm you ...

... but to reveal Christ in you.

*We carry this treasure in jars of clay ...*

— 2 Corinthians 4:7 —

God uses cracked vessels to leak His glory unto all those gathered around.

*Sometimes:*

• The collapse of your plan reveals the strength of His purpose.

• The pain you walk through becomes the oil you pour out.

• Your tears become the water that softens other people's hardened hearts.

You can lead from the pulpit with excellence ... but a true servant leader leads from wounds gained through the authenticity of experience.

## Fiery Application:

If leadership hasn't broken you yet … stay in it a little longer.

It's not a sign that you're failing.

It's a sign that God is trusting you with more weight.

- Let Him break your pride.

- Let Him break your self-sufficiency.

- Let Him break your image addiction.

And then let Him use the broken pieces to build something holy.

## Bold Declaration:

I will continue to hold to the towel of servant leadership even when that leadership breaks me.

## A Prayer for the Wounded Leader:

*Jesus, I've been hurt while holding the towel.*

*Betrayed while pouring. Burnt out while being faithful.*

*But I give it all back to You.*

*Heal the cracks in my heart, the fatigue in my soul, and the ache in my spirit.*

*Make me dangerous again — not because I'm whole, but because I'm surrendered.*

# — 7 —

# Leading from
# the Shadows

---

## The Glory of Obscure Faithfulness

*Your Father, who sees what is done in
secret, will reward you.*

— Matthew 6:4 —

## The Pain of Obscurity:

- You've prayed fervently.

- You're served faithfully.

- You've given sacrificially.

**And yet ...**

- No one noticed.

- No one clapped.

- No one said thank you.

Welcome to the shadows — where God does His deepest work.

Let's be clear: *Obscurity is not punishment.* **It's preparation.**

God does His best work in the dark:

- Moses spent 40 years in the desert before leading a nation.

- David was anointed king in private and then hidden in fields and caves.

- Jesus lived 30 quiet years before 3 years of public ministry.

So, if God has you in the shadows, He's shaping something sacred in you.

The world says: "Be visible."

The Spirit says: "Be available in the hidden place."

### The Dirty Work Builds Eternal Reward

The world values spotlights.

Heaven values basins.

*Think about it:*

- That usher who picks up trash after service?

- That greeter who shows up 30 minutes early in freezing weather?

- That kid's ministry volunteer who missed every sermon but changed diapers for Jesus?

They're shaking hell and heaven – quietly!

### Obscurity is Not a Curse – It's a Crown

*Better is one day in Your courts than a thousand elsewhere.*

— Psalm 84:10 —

The Psalmist says: "I'd rather be a doorkeeper …"

Translation: "Give me hidden faithfulness over hollow fame any day."

God is not looking for celebrity Christians – He's looking for consistent servants.

You don't need to be famous to be fruitful.

I once imagined what Heaven's version of the Oscars would look like:

- No red carpets

- No spotlights

- No speeches

Instead, Jesus walks to the stage and says:

*Where is the grandmother who prayed every morning at 4 A.M. for revival?*

*Where is the janitor who anointed chairs before anyone showed up?*

*Where is the single mom who tithed with a widow's mite and served at the food pantry?*

**All heaven roars in applause.**

The applause you may have missed out on while on earth is waiting for you in eternity.

You may never sit at the head table.

You may never preach at a conference, go viral, or have your ministry trend.

But if you've served in the shadows — you make heaven smile.

God counts:

- Hidden tears
- Late-night prayers
- Silent sacrifices

The last shall be first. The unseen shall be honored.

**Pray with me:**

*Lord, thank You for leading me into the dark places of service.*

*I desire to be visible to You but invisible to the world. I desire my applause to be heard in Heaven and not on this earth.*

*Let me pick up the trash.*

*Let me be the doorkeeper.*

*Let me be the volunteer that gives up the spotlight to achieve ministry for You.*

*I offer You my hidden tears, late-night prayers and silent sacrifices so that others may know You in all Your glory and goodness.*

# — 8 —

# The Basin and the Blood

---

**When Serving Costs You Everything**

*This is my blood, poured out for many ...*

— Mark 14:24 —

This is Jesus, the true servant leader. His towel was His life, and He offered it to all for salvation.

*He poured water into a basin and began to wash the disciples' feet ...*

— John 13:5 —

### The Cross Wasn't an Accident — It Was a Pattern

The towel and the cross were never separate.

- The basin wasn't stage drama.

- The blood wasn't accidental.

In one chapter …

*Jesus washes feet.*

In the next …

*He's dripping blood.*

This is the paradox of true leadership in God's kingdom: First the towel, then the thorns.

### The Basin is Beautiful … Until It Requires Blood

When Jesus knelt with that basin, He was doing more than cleaning dirt — He was modeling destiny.

He was saying:

"This is what leadership looks like. It gets lower. It cleans mess. It doesn't flinch at filth."

But He didn't stop there.

Love carried Him from the basin to Gethsemane, and from Gethsemane to Golgotha.

# The Cost of Kingdom Service

Servant leadership will:

- Break your routine.

- Drain your energy.

- Test your motives.

- Challenge your comfort.

- Sometimes cost you blood.

Ministry doesn't just ask for your gift – it asks for your guts.

I met a pastor who preaching revival with an IV bag attached to his arm during chemotherapy.

He said, "If Jesus bled for me, I can bleed for them."

That's what poured-out leadership looks like.

- It's not polished.

- It's not glamorous.

- But it's sacred.

Everyone wants the basin moment – few are willing to follow it to the bloody garden.

- Can I serve when it hurts?

- Can I love when it's not returned?

- Can I lead when no one applauds?

*Real leaders don't run from pain.*

They bleed in prayer, sweat in service, and cry in the night — but they stay the course.

## Jesus Didn't Just Serve the Deserving

Think of whose feet He washed:

- Peter, who would deny Him

- Judas, who would betray Him

- Thomas, who would doubt Him

- The rest, who would scatter from Him

Still, He poured water into a basin.

He still loved with open veins.

Servant leadership doesn't require others to deserve it. It requires you to deliver it.

Are you willing to:

- Preach after you've been misunderstood?

- Mentor someone who might fail you?

- Wash feet that might walk away from you?

Take your cue from the example of Jesus.

Step into His footprints today.

Offer your body, your blood, and your sacrifice for the underserving.

Hear Him smile and say, "You are learning, and I am proud of you."

### Prayer of the Poured-Out Leader:

*Jesus, You didn't just serve — You bled.*

*You didn't just give — You gave everything.*

*If the cost of love is blood, teach me to love anyway.*

*Break me of comfort. Deliver me from self-preservation.*

*Pour me out like oil until the basin of my calling is full.*

*I do not want cheap influence — I want holy impact.*

# — 9 —

# Towels Over Titles

---

### Redefining Greatness in the Local Church

*The greatest among you will be your servant.*

— Matthew 23:11 —

This was a problem in Jesus' day ...

*And it continues today ...*

Greatness needed to be redefined.

# Church Culture: Titles on the Door, but Towels on the Floor?

We've got more titles in the Church than ever before:

- Lead Pastor

- Executive Pastor

- Creative Director

- Worship Architect

- Intergalactic Apostle to the Nations

There's nothing wrong with titles. But here's the reality:

- Titles without towels leads to towers of ego.

- Towels without titles build the Kingdom.

Jesus never rebuked positions — He rebuked pride within positions.

## The Church Doesn't Need More Bosses. It Needs More Basins.

*Picture this:*

A sanctuary filled with leaders ...

*But no one jockeying for position ...*

Instead, everyone grabbing towels, cleaning wounds, praying in corners, and stacking chairs.

**Now that's revival.**

Because a church that values the basin will never be empty of His presence.

There was an old janitor in a church here in South Texas. No title. No mic. No applause.

Every Saturday night, he would crawl into the empty baptistry, kneel, and cry out:

"God, let these waters stir with salvation tomorrow."

No one knew.

But when dozens were saved every month, pastors wondered what the secret was.

They found him in the basin ... not the boardroom.

If you want a healthy staff culture, build it on towels, not thrones.

- Before your next meeting, gather together and

wash each other's feet.

- Before your next title upgrade, ask who you've discipled.

- Before your next platform moment, ask who you carried.

What's heavier to you — your title ... or your towel?

## What If Ministry Metrics Changed?

*Instead of:*

- "How many attended?"

- "How big is your budget?

- "How many campuses?"

*We asked:*

- "How many tears have been caught?"

- "How many burdens have been lifted?"

- "How many towels were used this week?"

Because Heaven isn't measuring your reach ...

*It's measuring your knees.*

## The Unlikely Servant Leaders

### Stephen:

*A deacon, not an apostle – stoned while preaching truth.*

### Phoebe:

*Called a "servant" of the church in Cenchreae – trusted by Paul.*

### Onesimus:

*A runaway slave – called "a dear brother" and a servant.*

None of them had massive pulpits.

But they made the pages of eternity.

You'll never love your platform more than when you've loved your people better.

### Declaration:

*We must become a towel church. We must serve. We must stoop. We must stay low. We must look like Jesus.*

**Pray with me:**

*Lord, strip us of performance.*

*Kill the addition to applause.*

*Rewire our DNA to reflect Yours — low, loyal, and loving.*

*May every usher, worship leader, kids' volunteer, administrator, and senior pastor be marked by a towel.*

*We declare: Our identity is not in our title but in Your towel.*

*Help us be the kind of church where people say, "I felt washed just by being there."*

# — 10 —

# From Applause to Assignment

---

## Overcoming the Addiction to Being Seen

*Be careful not to practice your righteous-
ness in front of others to be seen by them ...*

— Matthew 6:1 —

### When applause becomes a drug:

- You post the sermon clip.

- You wait for the likes.

- You refresh the feed.

- You scan the comments.

**But what happens when:**

- No one shares it?

- No one applauds you?

- No one invites you?

Do you still burn with the same fire?

Because the test of true leadership is not how you serve when you're celebrated ... but how you serve when you're unseen.

We preach servant leadership – but secretly crave spotlight validation.

We say, "To God be the glory" – but inwardly check our follower count.

**Here's the truth bomb:**

- If you need claps to keep going, you're not serving – you're performing.

- Applause feeds the ego – assignment feeds the

Spirit.

Let's break it down:

## Applause Driven

- Seeks crowds

- Needs reaction

- Stops when unseen

- Competes for influence

## Assignment Driven

- Seeks obedience

- Needs God's voice

- Stays faithful in silence

- Completes the mission

Jesus didn't chase clout.

He chased crosses.

He avoided fame and embraced assignment.

There was a young preacher who filled stadiums at 22.

At 30, he disappeared from the scene, burned out,

bitter and broke.

One night in prayer, he cried, "God, why did You let my ministry fail?"

The Lord whispered:

"You built a platform I never assigned. I called you to be a basin, not a billboard."

That man now leads a small church and has never felt more fulfilled.

Kill the need to be seen!

Slay the idol of applause!

Ask yourself daily:

- "Would I still preach this sermon if no one posted it?"

- "Would I still lead worship if no one tagged me?"

- "Would I still serve in this role if I'm never recognized?"

Ministry for man's praise is empty.

Ministry from God's assignment never runs dry.

Jesus lived for assignment, not applause:

- He withdrew when they tried to crown Him.

- He was silent before His accusers.

- He rode in on a donkey, not a war horse.

- He died to the sound of mockery, not cheers.

And yet … He completed His assignment.

**An anthem for assignment:**

- I am not addicted to applause.

- I am anchored in assignment.

- Likes don't define me.

- Comments don't validate me.

- Obedience is my oxygen.

- Jesus is my reward.

**Pray with me:**

*Father, deliver me from hunger for crowds.*

*Detox me from addiction to affirmation.*

*Let me lead like Jesus — silent when necessary, obedient always.*

*I lay down every idol of attention and pick up the towel of assignment.*

*Whether it's in front of ten or ten thousand, I will serve for Your smile alone.*

# — II —

# The Weight of the Towel

---

**Servant Leadership Isn't Always Glorious**

- Sometimes it's draining.

- Sometimes it's lonely.

- Sometimes it's invisible.

When the applause fades and each thank you dries up, that towel can feel like a burden.

## The Reality of Thankless Service

- You stayed late, no one noticed.

- You counseled a hurting soul, no one thanked you.

- You gave sacrificially, no one reciprocated.

- You prayed relentlessly, no one saw your tears.

It's tempting to quit. To walk away.

## Biblical Examples of Thankless Servants:

- Noah worked 120 years building an ark for a world that mocked him.

- Elijah ran for his life after serving God faithfully.

- Paul faced beatings, shipwrecks, and imprisonment — and often wrote letters asking for prayer support.

None of these servants quit.

Your reward isn't always immediate.

Your labor isn't always applauded.

*But it is seen by the One who counts every tear*

*and every act of faithfulness.*

- Keep picking up the towel.

- Endurance grows character.

- Character grows hope.

- Hope never disappoints.

*When the towel feels heavy, remember:*

- You are not alone.

- You are not forgotten.

- You are on a path paved by every faithful servant before you.

**Pray this Declaration of Perseverance:**

*I will not grow weary. I will serve quietly. I will love without applause.*

*I will carry the towel of servanthood until the harvest comes.*

*Jesus, You understood what it means to be weary. Strengthen me when I'm tired.*

*Encourage me when I feel unseen. Renew my heart to keep serving faithfully.*

*Let Your presence be my rest and reward.*

# — 12 —

# The Final Seat

---

### Receiving the Crown of Servanthood

*Well done, good and faithful servant! You have been faithful with a few things; I will put you in charge of many things.*

— Matthew 25:21 —

We chase earthly seats — head tables, front rows, VIP lounges.

But Jesus promises a far greater reward: a crown of

righteousness for those who serve faithfully.

The highest seat of honor isn't on earth.

It's at His right hand in Heaven.

### Jesus' Promises to Servants

- Not applause, but approval

- Not fame, but favor

- Not temporary honor, but eternal glory

The crown Jesus offers isn't for rulers who lord over others.

It's for those who …

- Picked up towels

- Washed feet

- Loved without spotlight

It's a crown shaped by …

- Humility

- Faithfulness

- Sacrifice

- Love

**Imagine heaven's throne room:**

The King Himself places a crown on a servant's head, not one of gold or jewels, but a towel-shaped diadem — a symbol of sacrificial love and service.

The applause across the Kingdom is thunderous — echoing through eternity.

## Taking a Seat Beside Our Lord

We can choose Christ. We can choose servant-hood. We can choose His crown and not the world's.

- Live for the applause that lasts beyond the grave.

- Serve with the towel that points to the throne.

- When you pick up that towel, you're not losing status — you're gaining a crown.

**Pray with me:**

*Lord Jesus, thank You for the towel You carried.*

*Help me to live for Your approval, not man's applause.*

*May I one day hear You say, "Well, done, good and faithful servant."*

*Until then, I'll serve with joy, love with passion, and lead with humility.*

*In Your matchless name, Amen.*

— 13 —

# The Cost of Leadership

---

## The Price of Position on the Family

*For if someone does not know how to manage his own household, how will he care for God's church?*

— I Timothy 3:5 —

Ministry is a sacred calling — but it is also a sacrificial one.

While pastors and ministry leaders willingly lay

down their lives for the sake of the Gospel, it's often their families who feel the weight of that sacrifice most deeply.

This chapter is not a complaint. It is not an indictment.

It is a confession.

It is also an invitation to recognize the hidden cost of spiritual leadership, particularly on our homes; and to courageously realign our priorities with both Heaven's call and our family's needs.

### When the Pulpit Becomes a Prison

There's a danger in being celebrated publicly and disconnected privately.

Pastors often wear smiles that mask exhaustion.

We pour out Sunday after Sunday, midweek after midweek, wedding after funeral, while our spouses and children quietly hunger for a piece of what we freely give to others.

*Sometimes we even sacrifice our marriages on the altar of ministry.*

We convince ourselves it's for the Kingdom, that

the church needs us, that revival can't wait ... but our first ministry is to our family.

If the pulpit becomes a place that isolates us from our home ...

Then it's no longer a platform for God's glory.

It's no longer a place we practice servanthood but a prison we've willingly entered.

Don't gain the world and lose your soul.

Don't pick up the towel to grow the church and lose your children.

True servanthood serves your family first.

### The Unseen Pressure on Pastoral Families

*Ministry families often live under a microscope. They face criticism over ...*

- Every action

- Every word

- Every absence

*They are:*

- Evaluated

- Dismembered

- Judged

The children of pastors don't just carry their own name, they struggle under the weight of yours. They didn't sign up for the spotlight, yet they often live in it.

*Spouses have their own challenges as they become:*

- Unpaid assistants

- Emotional shock-absorbers

- Silent intercessors

They sit alone on Sunday mornings when their partner is "on duty," and often manage the home in the absence of their shepherd.

The family becomes a mirror, reflecting the leader's weariness, driven pace and emotional residue.

We must ask ourselves, are we bringing peace home to our family, or just the leftovers from our duties to the Church?

A pastor once confessed, "I gave the church 30 years of my life and only realized at my retirement party that I'd missed 30 years of dinner at my own table."

## Balancing Calling and Covenant

God never called you to win the world and lose your home.

The same God who called you into ministry also instituted family. And He never pits one against the other.

If you feel torn between church and home, it's not always a sign to abandon the call – it may be a sign to adjust your rhythm.

- Let your calendar reflect your covenant.

- Prioritize what cannot be delegated – your marriage, your children, your home.

- Anyone can preach your sermon in a pinch, but no one else can be your child's parent or your spouse's partner.

- Sunday mornings aren't just for the church – they are for your family too.

The health of your ministry will never exceed the health of your home.

# Guardrails for the Minister's Home

*Schedule sacred time.*

- Date nights

- Family days

- Digital sabbaths

Make appointments with your family that carry the same weight as an elder board meeting.

These aren't luxuries … they are lifelines.

Your top job is to protect the dinner table.

*Plan times to eat together …*

- Without phones

- Without meetings

- Without sermon prep

It's one of the most sacred altars you'll ever build.

*Let the Church see your humanity.*

- Be transparent.

- Don't pretend to be perfect.

- Let your family be human.

When the church sees that you value your home, you begin to model a healthy faith that transcends performance.

*Invite your family into your ministry.*

Involve them, yes. Force them, no. Let them serve because they want to, not because they feel they must bear your mantle.

*Always remember that no matter what's shaken your family, redemption is still possible.*

If you've made mistakes, if your marriage feels distant, or your children feel overlooked, it's not too late. The God of the pulpit is also the God of your living room.

*God wants your family renewed.*

- Ask forgiveness.
- Gather with your family.
- Invite healing – for everyone.
- Begin again as a family.

The goal isn't to be a famous preacher.

The goal is to be a faithful husband, a loving wife,

a present father, a nurturing mother … and yes, a devoted servant of the Lord.

*Let your family be your legacy, not your regret.*

**Pray with me:**

*Lord, help me to carry the weight of my calling without crushing the ones closest to me.*

*Teach me how to lead my home as faithfully as I lead the Church.*

*Let my family be my truest joy, not my justification that pulls me from them.*

*And let my legacy not be the sermons I preached, but the lives I loved well, with my family above everyone else.*

*In Jesus' name, amen.*

# A Final Word

You can find Tim on the South Texas District website at www.stxag.org, on Facebook, or at his Houston office when he's not traveling his home state ministering in the churches across the South Texas District.

He'd be thrilled to connect with you and share stories of God's faithfulness.

# Additional Books by
# Tim R. Barker

If you liked this book, you may be interested in additional books Tim has written. Turn the page for a short description of each book. All are available on Amazon.

# My *Jesus* Journey

This soul-building, introspective 4-book series reveals Tim's innermost heart on subjects that affect all of us, from Cooperation to Loyalty to The Truth of Salvation and more.

The books in this series include:

*My Jesus Journey*

*My Jesus Journey: Crescendo*

*My Jesus Journey: Glissando*

*My Jesus Journey: Rhapsody*

# At *Your* Feet

In this book, you will read of God's favor and His redemption, for you are chosen and forgiven. In Jesus, you can find the rest you desire, for at His feet, His joy becomes whole.

Come to Jesus today. He holds His hand out to you.

# from the Book of Hebrews

# The Lord with Us

Do you have a relationship with Jesus? The rewards are great, but if we fail to heed the warnings in the Word, the consequences are also great.

Even if we call ourselves Christian, we must live according to God's will. The Lord is with us when we walk with Him. This is the message from the book of Hebrews.

# Our Privilege of Joy

*A Study of the Book of Philippians*

Philippians is our blueprint from the Father, our plan for joy. It was written by the hand of Paul during his time in a Roman prison, but the voice is the Father's, entreating us to lift our hands in praise to Him, and to find joy even in the difficult parts of our lives.

# NAMES
## OF GOD

Our name tells people who we are.

What about the name Christian? That's what the followers of Jesus call themselves. What information can people glean about us when we put a fish symbol on the bumper of our car, or we wear a cross around our neck? And, importantly, do our actions live up to their expectations?

This book is an in-depth teaching about the ten names of God.

# THE VISION OF
# NEHEMIAH
## GOD'S PLAN FOR RIGHTEOUS LIVING

The Book of Nehemiah reveals a vital truth that our instant society often overlooks. Determination can take us only so far in achieving the goals God has for today's Church.

Winning the lost for Christ takes preparation in both our time and our finances. We become the "right stuff" for achieving God's plan when we are willing to risk everything for Him.

# GOD'S REVELATION AND YOUR FUTURE

The book of Revelation is first and foremost a revelation about Jesus, not just the future.

John reveals Christ as the King of Glory, the conqueror, the one in charge of history, the one who alone controls the future, controls the nations, controls all the universe! This is the Jesus who is coming!

The book of Revelation shows us the glorified Christ and the certainty of His ruling over all things. We are not stumbling toward an uncertain future, but we must be in fellowship with the King!

# Truth, Love & Redemption

### The Holy Spirit For Today

There is no greater empowerment for the Christian of today than to seek out the Holy Spirit. It was considered vital in the early days of Christendom. Now, many times it is pushed aside as "for then" and not "for now."

We are in greater need of the truth, love, and redemption that flows from an encounter with the Holy Spirit than ever before. The Scriptures tell us that our realization of our need for Christ flows from the Spirit. Even before we accept Christ, the Holy Spirit draws us to Him.

# The Call of Ephesians

**Building the Church of Today**

Paul understood that legalism can become a hindrance to our Christian walk and that we must focus on Christ and Christ alone. When our faith hits the road, God is there with us. He challenges us to trust Him to walk at our side through every challenge we might face.

When we do, we become mighty warriors in God's army.

That's Paul's message in a nutshell, and it's vital we take it to heart.

# The Twelve
## Taking up the Mantle of Christ

Twelve men were chosen to fulfill Christ's legacy on the earth.

Eleven looked to Jesus for the answers to life's questions. One chose the world and the world failed him.

These men were as varied as the members of our modern church, at times at odds with one another, but forged by Jesus into a single unit that overcame everything the devil could throw at them. What lesson can we learn from them?

Our only option is to choose Christ.

# END TIMES

Scripture provides us a timeline of events that signal that the end is coming soon.

1. The Church Age
2. The Rapture of the Church
3. The Tribulation
4. The Second Coming of Jesus Christ
5. The Millennium
6. The Great White Throne Judgment
7. New Heavens and New Earth

Follow along through each of these Biblical timeline events.

# Anticipating the Return of Christ

Are we waiting or are we watching for His appearance in the skies? The difference is in being ready for His return and risking missing Him altogether.

This book covers six areas of preparation for the Return of Christ.

1. Waiting
2. Mindful
3. Joyful
4. Praying
5. Thanking
6. Faithful.

Are you anticipating Christ's return? I am.

# I*Your*nvitation to Christ

Your Invitation to Christ guarantees six things. Once you accept Christ's invitation you can:

1. Rest. It's yours in the midst of whatever comes your way.

2. See. Your eyes are opened to the supernatural.

3. Follow. Christ is your only true leader.

4. Drink. The ambrosia of Jesus becomes yours.

5. Dine. You will find renewal in your fellowship with your Lord.

6. Inherit. The Kingdom will one day be yours. It's called Heaven.

Salvation comes through Christ. God desires our presence, and we draw closer to Him through our Lord and Savior, Jesus.

# The Authentic Christian

**Revealing Christ through the Fruit of the Spirit**

How do we prove who we say we are?

What's the secret to how it's done?

Is it in appearance? Actions that portray honesty?

How do we live out our Christian example, prove that we are who we say we are? What's our authentication, our password, our photo ID?

That's what this book is about, how we can live a real and honest Christian life that reflects the truth of Jesus living through us.

When you finish this book, you will understand what it means to be an authentic Christian.

# UNIFIED CHURCH

The world cries out for your leadership as a Christ-driven example of how to find security and safety in Him.

We must band together arm-in-arm, hand-in-hand, our thoughts, compassion, and commitment to each other linked for a common goal we all share: spreading the message of salvation to a world that desperately needs to see the example of Jesus lived out through committed believers.

This book will become a useful tool to focus your witness to those around you and strengthen your relationship to your family, your involvement in your local body of believers and your commitment to Christ.

# Mighty Men of Courage
## From the Bible

Joseph who was sold into slavery. Daniel faced the lion's den. Abraham saw few of the promises of God during his lifetime. Moses lived for four decades in disgrace, an apparent failure.

Elijah hid in the desert with the ravens for three years, and Paul was arrested for his faith and thrown in prison. Repeatedly.

Yet today we recognize these men as courageous examples of faith in God. The difference is that they took a stand for God, looked beyond their personal circumstances and in faith allowed the hand of God to lead them.

Christ is calling. I want to answer.

Join me today, won't you?

# Open
## Doors

Inside or outside. That's what a door conveys.

We can choose to stand on one side or the other. We can keep things inside or outside, open the door or close it. Some doors are found in opportunities, worship, or faithfulness. Then there are emotional doors. We can be locked in or out. The doors become prison bars, trapping us in painful situations.

Death is the final door in this life. Do you dread it or look forward to what's on the other side?

This book is your opportunity to discover how the doors in your life align with the Word of God. The choice is yours: inside or outside?

Decide for Jesus today. He is the only choice worth making. Christ is calling.

I want to answer. Join me today, won't you?

# Reflecting Christ

—— through the ——

# Fruit
## of the
# Spirit

The reflection we cast. Does it reveal us or Christ?

There is a distinction between outward appearances and true substance, and it's clear in how we live out our lives as followers of Jesus.

Why would the world accept a Christian who doesn't live like Christ? That's where the Fruit of the Spirit comes into play in our lives.

How do we know the Fruit is active in our lives? We see it in the love we show to those in need.

Decide for Jesus today. He is the only choice worth making.

# CALLED CAMP
## —2025—

Moses ... freeing the Egyptian slaves and parting the Red Sea!

David ... the King and the Psalmist!

Then there's Gideon, Jonah and Jeremiah!

Each of these men had to start somewhere small: Moses ran away to live in the desert. David tended sheep. Gideon, Jonah and Jeremiah just hoped to be left alone!

What has God called you to do for the kingdom? Are you willing to say yes?

Decide for Jesus today. He is the only choice worth making.

# Discovering
# GOD
### in the
# Secret
# Places

The Word reveals to us that we will never have all the answers. God has set boundaries on our knowledge.

What seems right and appropriate for us, our families, and those we affect is based on feelings, circumstances, and the emotions that drive us to react rather than to reason.

We cry, "Where are you, God?" He whispers to us, "Slow down, and you will find me."

As you read this book, challenge yourself. Choose Wonder over Worry, bask in God's Season, and let the calendar of your life be written by the One who delivers us from a life of sin and shame.

Choose to trust in God, for He is the only one deserving of our eternal adoration.

www.ingramcontent.com/pod-product-compliance
Lightning Source LLC
Chambersburg PA
CBHW052114090426
42741CB00009B/1810